W9-ANN-687

Let's Talk About Good Manners

Diane Shaughnessy

The Rosen Publishing Group's
PowerKids Press™
New York

Published in 1997 by The Rosen Publishing Group, Inc.
29 East 21st Street, New York, NY 10010

First Edition

Book Design: Erin McKenna

Photo Illustrations: Cover and all photo illustrations by Ira Fox.

Shaughnessy, Diane.
    Let's talk about good manners / Diane Shaughnessy.
        p. cm. — (The let's talk library)
    Includes index.
    Summary: A simple discussion of what good manners are, why good manners are important, and how manners are different in different cultures.
    ISBN 0-8239-5045-X
    1. Etiquette for children and teenagers. [1. Etiquette.] I. Title. II. Series.
BJ1857.C5S44 1997
395.1'22—dc21
                                              96-39984
                                                  CIP
                                                      AC

Manufactured in the United States of America

Table of Contents

Taryn, Kara, and Trey

Taryn had her hands full of videotapes. "Kara, open the door!" she yelled to her sister. Kara didn't even look up from the book she was reading. Their brother, Trey, came into the room with his hands full of cookies. "Kara, will you please open the door? My hands are full."

Kara said, "Sure." She got up and opened the door. Trey said, "Thanks," and gave her a cookie for helping him. Taryn realized that she hadn't been very **polite** (poh-LYT) to Kara. She hadn't used good manners.

◀ If you use good manners, people are more likely to help you.

What Are Good Manners?

Good manners are ways of being polite to other people. Using good manners shows someone that you **respect** (ree-SPEKT) him or her. It also shows that you care about that person's feelings. Using good manners helps make everyone's life a little easier. When people know how to act with each other, they are less likely to hurt each other's feelings. By using good manners, you are treating other people the way you would like them to treat you.

In the United States, it is polite to shake hands when you meet someone new. ▶

Learning Good Manners

People learn good manners from their families and friends. Listen to the way your family members treat each other. You will probably hear the words "please," "thank you," and "I'm sorry."

But just because your brother never says "thank you" after you give him something doesn't mean you should stop saying "thank you." Do the things that make people feel good, not the things that make people feel bad.

◀ We learn good manners from our friends and family.

When to Use Good Manners

It is always right to use good manners. When you say "please," you show that you know you are asking someone for something. When you say "thank you," you show that you are **grateful** (GRAYT-ful) for something someone has given you. When you say "I'm sorry," you show that you know you did something wrong, and that you will try hard not to do it again.

But there are different manners for different times. Let's go over what some of those manners are and why they are important.

When someone doesn't use good manners, he makes other people feel bad. ▶

Good Manners at School

You share your school with a lot of people. Schools have many rules. Some of these, such as no running in the halls, no fighting, and no food fights, help keep the students safe.

Others, such as being on time, help people get along. If you are late to school, you **disrupt** (dis-RUPT) the class when you come into the room. If you talk while the teacher is talking, you won't hear what she says. You may miss something important. It is helpful to everyone if students use good manners in school.

◀ When you talk during class, you disrupt the class.

Good Manners at the Table

People eat together all the time—at dinner, in the school lunchroom, and at someone else's house. You notice the way other people eat. They notice the way that *you* eat, too. If you talk with your mouth full, no one can understand what you're saying. If you reach across the table for the salt, you may knock something over. Instead, ask for someone to please pass you the salt. Meals are a time for families and friends to share what they have been doing. Don't **interrupt** (inter-UPT) when other people are talking. You want them to listen when you are talking, don't you?

It is polite to ask for something to be ▶
passed to you at the table.

Getting Along with Others

Good manners help you get along with other people. One important good manner is **sharing** (SHAYR-ing). Sometimes you may want to do something that someone else is doing. You may want to take that toy or game away from your friend. But a person with good manners would say, "May I play with that when you are done?" In the same way, if a friend wants to play with one of your toys, it's good manners to share your toy or game with him. Sharing tells your friend that you care about him and want him to enjoy your toys, too.

◀ When you share, you are using good manners.

17

Kim and Lee

Kim handed her video game to Lee. "Here," she said. "You can play with it first."

"Thanks. My brother never lets me play with his video games. I don't like to play with him anymore," said Lee. Kim was glad that she shared her game with Lee. She knew that being a good friend meant sharing. She also knew that by sharing with Lee, she was showing Lee how to treat her. Having good manners helped Kim and Lee get along well.

Sharing tells the other person that you care about him. ▶

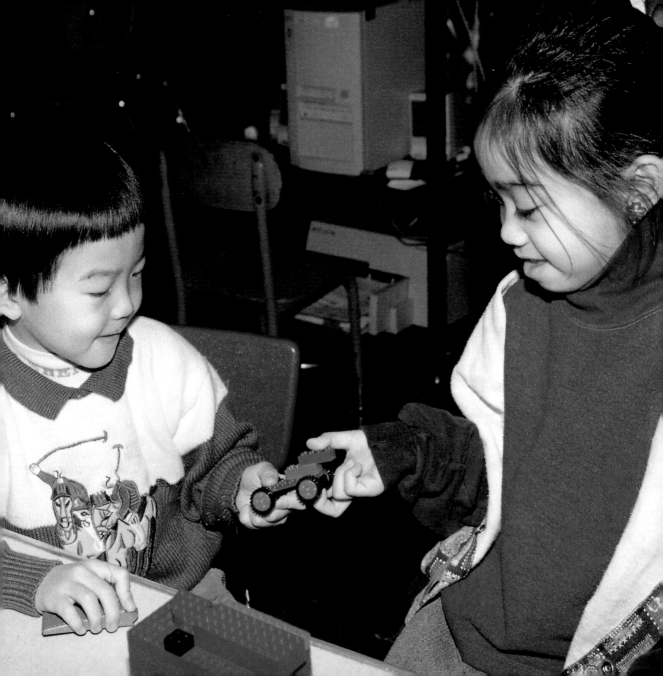

Being Rude

Not everyone has good manners. Some people forget to say "thank you." Others may interrupt you when you're talking. And some people never say "I'm sorry." When a person doesn't use good manners, he is being **rude** (ROOD). When someone is rude, he may hurt someone else's feelings.

Just because some people don't have good manners doesn't mean it's okay for *you* not to use good manners. Treat those people the way you want them to treat you—politely.

◀ Good manners help people get along.

21

Different Kinds of Manners

There are many **cultures** (KUL-cherz) in the world. Each culture has its own set of good manners. In Japan, it is polite to bow when you meet someone. If you visit Japan, you would bow to the Japanese people you meet. These good manners may be different from the good manners that you learn. But they **exist** (egg-ZIST) for the same reason—to be polite and show respect for other people.

Glossary

culture (KUL-cher) The customs, art, and ways of doing
    things for a certain group of people.

disrupt (dis-RUPT) To break up or cause disorder.

exist (egg-ZIST) To be.

grateful (GRAYT-ful) Feeling good because something
    nice was done to or for you.

interrupt (in-ter-UPT) To break in when people are talking
    or doing something.

polite (poh-LYT) Behaving properly or having good
    manners.

respect (ree-SPEKT) To honor someone or something.

rude (ROOD) Not polite or kind.

sharing (SHAYR-ing) Dividing something into parts and
    splitting between people or using something
    together.

Index